Gifts Guaranteed to Please a Woman
A Guide for Men©

Karen Adams

Illustrated by Chris Wrinn

© 2002 Karen Adams. All rights reserved.

No part of this book may be reproduced, stored in a retrieval system, or transmitted by any means, electronic, mechanical, photocopying, recording, or otherwise, without written permission from the author.

ISBN: 1-4033-4854-5 (electronic)
ISBN: 1-4033-4855-3 (softcover)

Library of Congress Control Number: 2002092882

This book is printed on acid free paper.

Printed in the United States of America
Bloomington, IN

Illustrated by Chris Wrinn

1stBooks – rev. 09/16/02

Table of Contents

Chapter *1* : General Principles 1

Rule Number 1 - Be Observant 3

Rule Number 2 - Timing is Everything 5

Rule Number 3 - Presentation Counts 6

Rule Number 4 - Buy Quality 7

Rule Number 5 - Make it Personal 8

Rule Number 6 - The Element of Surprise 9

Chapter *2* : Old Stand-bys 11
- *Flowers* 11
- *Candy* 18
- *Jewelry* 21
- *Perfumes* 27
- *Cards* 37
- *Lingerie* 38

Chapter *3* : Original Creations 43
- *Film* 43
- *The Written Word* 45
- *Painting* 48

Music 48
Things that Grow 49

Chapter 4: Special Events 51

Birthdays 51
Anniversary 55
Christmas/Hanukkah 57
Mother's Day 58
Valentine's Day 58
Job Well Done 60

Chapter 5: The Gift of an Experience 63

Trip Fantastic 63
Mind Expanding 67
Soul Searching 70
Body Improving 71

Chapter 6: Sweet Nothings - Sensual Pleasures 73

Massage 73
Bubble Bath 74
Exotic Dancing 76
Up Close and Personal 76
Love Slave 77
Hugs and Kisses 78

Chapter 7: Manners Matter 79

Cell Phone Etiquette
Dinner "Thank Yous"
Gift "Thank Yous"
Bedroom Manners

Chapter 8: So What's in a Salary? 83

Courting on a Student's Salary
Courting on a Postman's Salary
Courting on an Executive's Salary
Courting on a Trust Fund

Chapter 9: Saying "I Do" 89

Basic Principles 89
The Gift of Life 91
The Eternal Gift 94

Chapter 10: Times of Trauma 95

How to Deal with Illness 96
Mortality 98

Final Thoughts 99

Dedicated

To

Justin and Constance

Chapter *1*: General Principles

Chapter *1*

General Principles

A gift should be given from the heart with no strings attached. A gift should show effort and creativity. You get extra points if it hurts a little. By that I mean you have to give of your most precious possessions, whether it's time, money or both.

The "Ouch" Test

Did you recently buy yourself a new set of $1,000 Ping golf clubs but spent $30 on cologne for her birthday? How about your purchase of a super deluxe 500 watt sound system with speakers big enough to blast you out of the Hollywood Bowl? You "generously" gave her a

no-name silk scarf from a discount store (at least it could have been from *Hermès*). You have time to plan for the fishing trip with the guys and two hours a night to work out at the gym, but you didn't find time to make dinner reservations when you asked her out for Saturday night. These stories have a life of their own and in fact are passed on through word of mouth from girlfriend to girlfriend, sister to sister, mother to daughter. You don't want to become an infamous character in this tradition of oral history.

On the flip side, a well-conceived beautifully presented gift can earn major points for years to come. The price can be as small as a handful of out-of-season tulips or a simple breakfast in bed. A man who has mastered the art of giving is a rare and desirable creature. If you want to be worshipped and adored by the woman in your life, read on and become a legend in your own time.

Chapter 1: General Principles

Rule Number 1 - Be Observant

*S*ounds obvious but most men fail to pay attention to the details that make her unique. Come on guys . . . wake up! Doesn't the woman you care about deserve as much attention as your business? O.K., how about your hobby? The female is so much more observant and sensitive to your needs. She knows everything about your job, your favorite foods, the clothes you like. Ask any woman the size of her man's shirt or shoe size. I bet you don't know hers. I've seen women obsess about the right color or pattern of a tie. Of course she knows everything in your wardrobe to match it. She knows all your passions, your favorite sport right down to your favorite teams and brand of running shoe.

A girlfriend once told me how disappointed she was after receiving a Christmas present from her husband of 20 years. It was a day-glow yellow flowered print dress . . . something in which she would never be caught dead. He had forgotten to take the receipt out of the box, which confirmed he purchased it Christmas Eve on his way home from work, probably at the suggestion of the department store sales person. And all those years she wore pastel, solid classic clothes.

What a disappointment to think her husband was so insensitive not to notice her preference, not to recognize her unique style. She returned it the next day. Worse yet, he didn't even ask why she never wore the dress.

Chapter 1: General Principles

Rule Number 2 - *Timing is Everything*

Don't be late for any special event . . . birthday, anniversary, Valentine's Day. Short of a head-on collision or death in the family, there is no excuse. Gifts that arrive late are a great disappointment. If it's a gift like a concert or trip, allow time for her to plan. Don't make her choose between losing her job or a week cruising the Greek Isles. Plan ahead. Maybe you thought you could get away with that cheesy souvenir coffee mug you got in the airport gift shop. Guess again. Gifts that scream 'he bought me without any thought five minutes ago' enroll you in the gift givers Hall of Shame.

Gifts Guaranteed to Please a Woman

Rule Number *3* - Presentation Counts

*E*ven the most welcomed gift, if taken out of the bag with the price tag still on, is self-defeating. Wrapping is important. An inexpensive gift, beautifully wrapped, is much more exciting to open. If you can't figure this out, ask someone to help or buy from a store that wraps. Use satin ribbon. My favorite is French silk with a small wire on the edge to give shape to the bow. Wrapping paper should be something other than the ordinary. Museum gift shops sometimes sell Italian marbleized paper. Look in expensive bookstores; they sometimes sell unusual wrapping paper. Buy a cloth covered or china box in which to put your gift. This becomes a part of the gift itself. One exotic flower elegantly boxed in tissue and ribbon

counts more than two dozen cheap mums from the supermarket.

Chapter *1*: General Principles

Rule Number *4* - Buy Quality

*I*t is better to buy a small anything from a quality store than a big something from a cheap one. Anything from Tiffany's is fun to open. That little blue box with the white ribbon, even a key chain for $20, is better than a complete set of 12 imitation crystal goblets. Buy something precious, even if only in a small amount. Whether it be candy, caviar or flowers, buy the best you can afford.

Rule Number 5 - Make it Personal

This gift should be for her personal use. Don't be self-centered. The last thing your love wants is a book about fly fishing or football superheroes so she can get to know more about <u>your</u> favorite pastimes. I remember one friend who told me about a boyfriend who marked every special occasion with history books or paraphernalia from his native Finland so she could learn more about him! Thanks, but no thanks. The large-screen projection TV is a gift for the whole family, as opposed to the new cross-country skis for her personal use. Understand the difference. Then there was the anniversary gift of a riding lawnmower so they could share in cutting the lawn. Forget it. And that goes for household appliances . . . a vacuum is a gift of drudgery, not love.

Chapter *1*: General Principles

Rule Number *6* - The Element of Surprise

*I*f she can guess what it is before she opens it, you lose points for creativity. It's Christmas and there's a small package under the tree, "It must be another bottle of perfume I don't like." "If it's my birthday, it must be roses." The only time this is not clichéd is if you have been giving her roses for 25 years. Even then, you could add tickets to Hawaii to see where roses grow the entire year. Vary the gift or the packaging. Wrap a small piece of jewelry in a big box; weight it with a brick. That will be a welcome surprise.

Gifts Guaranteed to Please a Woman

*T*ry a new occasion for gift giving. How about a New Year's Day gift? Give her something to let her know you are looking forward to spending another wonderful year with your favorite person. Take 12 old photos of the two of you and make them into a calendar. A print shop can help you do this. It's relatively inexpensive and she can be reminded of the thoughtful gift for the next twelve months. Her girlfriends will "Ooh" and "Ahh" when she brings this to work.

*M*aster these six principles and you have graduated from Gift Giving 101. Now, onto the graduate courses…

Chapter 2: Old Stand-Bys

Chapter 2

Old Stand-Bys

Flowers

"Say it with love, say it with flowers" advises the FTD advertisement. A woman is always happy to receive flowers but there are degrees of happiness. When dealing with your average florist, there are pitfalls to avoid. A general rule of thumb is no mums, no carnations ... especially dyed. That went out with the high school prom corsage. And no average long-stem fragrant-less roses. Since florists seem to select flowers for longevity, they might as well be plastic. The FTD catalogue also features the favorite "roundy-moundy" arrangement found in hospital gift shops and airport vending machines. These unimaginative concoctions are always perfectly symmetrical and perfectly boring.

Gifts Guaranteed to Please a Woman

To discriminate between the typical arrangement and something more sophisticated there are a few universally recognized trade terms to be utilized. The opposite of "roundy-moundy" is "loose and airy". "No carnations or mums" immediately states to the florist that it is not to be traditional. The two together are a code for an upscale selection. Adding the phrase "Please use Holland flowers" may refine the choice to an even higher level. As you become more discerning, you must also add dollar signs. The buyer cannot expect to get a meaningful arrangement for $20-25. If money is an issue and even $25 will break your bank, stick to the one flower beautifully wrapped or a tiny bunch of violets. You get the same points for thoughtfulness. Remember to write your own card and give it to the florist. Too often, no matter how many times you spell the name, it still ends up wrong on the florist's card.

English or European garden style is another alternative to the clichéd selections in the florist catalogue. This is a selection of flowering and green small potted plants in a basket. Prolonged life and easy care make it a great gift. In some parts of the country, especially small, rural areas, it might be confused with a "dishgarden". Be careful, this could be a cactus in a bowl. Don't leave it to chance; be specific.

One way of getting something special is to find a florist that is also a garden center. If it is during the months from early spring through summer, you can give a long lasting plant that may be more

Chapter 2: Old Stand-Bys

meaningful than cut flowers. For instance: topiary fairy rose bushes, 3-foot standard rose trees in a terra cotta container, fuchsia, geranium, lilacs or hydrangeas. If necessary, be sure you include planting costs in the price. What a woman doesn't need is a gift with more labor involved!

You definitely get more flowers for your money with loose-cut bouquets. Be sure to add a few dollars for an elegant bow and you'll have a truly gorgeous gift. Things to remember when giving fresh cut flowers: Number 1 - she must condition and arrange them herself. Two dozen tulips can easily be put in a glass bowl with a little powdered preservative, but a complicated selection of roses, lilies, fuchsia, etc. requires that a container be chosen and stems must be freshly cut to absorb water and artfully arranged. This can be a problem if you are on your way to the theater or if she is about to welcome 20 of her best friends to a dinner party. In which case, she probably has already purchased and arranged her flowers for the evening. When sending fresh flowers out of town, to a hotel or to a resort, make sure someone is there to receive them. I once came back from a wonderful evening to my hotel room to find a fortune in wilted flowers wrapped elegantly in cellophane and ribbon on my bed. Too bad they had been left out of water for four hours and were almost dead. What a waste!

The more sophisticated the woman, the more discerning you must be. Even commonly overused flowers come in a more creative variety.

- **Roses**

When sending roses, you should insist they be transported in water tubes. This will prolong their life. The most commonly given rose is the fragrant-less, long-stem, red hybrid tea. If you have been giving your wife these every year on your anniversary for 20 years, don't stop. She'll worry. Other than that situation, why be one of the common unimaginative masses? A creative father gave his wife one rose for every ounce that each of their children weighed at birth. The trend-setting floral designers - the ones who write the books, give the lectures and are on the talk show circuit - would suggest floribundas, polyanthus and other varieties of shrub or spray roses. These species have more than one bloom on the stem. They look like small bouquets, are more unpredictable, more natural, less contrived than the long stem rose. This type is more suggestive of a real garden - moving, bending, sinuous. A neighbor of mine gave his wife a beautiful old-fashioned tea rose bush (very fragrant) every year for their anniversary. They now have a beautiful rose garden that celebrates their 25 years of marriage.

Seek something out of the ordinary. If your florist won't cooperate, get a new florist. Roses are packaged to the retailer in twenty-fives (two dozen plus one for breakage.) If you want something different, special order more than a dozen so the vendor doesn't "eat" more

Chapter *2*: Old Stand-Bys

than a few flowers. Order early to facilitate the availability. In France, they only give odd numbers of flowers because of sensitivity for balanced arrangements. The only exception is a dozen roses (the thirteenth is for his lapel.)

Here are some "don'ts" with roses: Don't use baby's breath as filler. It is just too, too trite. There are so many other good fillers such as Queen Anne's Lace, Monte Casino, Wax Flower, Misty Blue, Scotch Broom, Lemon Leaves, and so on. Don't buy your roses from the grocery store. The only statement that makes is you stopped for beer and potato chips and the flowers were an afterthought.

- **Lilies**

Symbolic of devotion, these lovely flowers are fragrant and long lasting. Remember to remove the orange powder on the stamens as they open, because they can permanently stain anything they touch. We will assume the florist has prepared the ones already opened when you purchased them.

- **Orchids**

This rare flower is for the rare woman. It is prized for its delicate bloom, which may last for several months as long as you don't over-water them.

- **Tulips**

Always buy in quantity . . . at least a dozen or two. French tulips, with curly edges, are preferable. They last longer and open more like a rose. Don't forget the copper penny in the water to keep them standing straight.

- **Carnations**

Forget it.

- **Mums**

Ditto! Unless it's autumn and you are buying potted plants en masse for color around the patio.

Chapter *2*: Old Stand-Bys

- **Flowers for the Kitchen**

*H*erbs are a plant you can eat. This is a great choice for the gourmet cook in your life. Baskets or terra cotta window planters filled with basil, chives, coriander, dill, curry, mint, oregano, parsley, sage, rosemary, and thyme. These plants can be kept in the kitchen or planted outside in the spring. She will think of you every time she flavors her recipes.

- **Flowers for the Bedroom**

*F*or the true romantic, a bed covered in rose petals is the ultimate luxury. This can get a little tricky to find from a florist. Of course, the easiest way to get a supply of petals is from a friend with a garden. Be careful with dark red on expensive sheets. Your body heat can create stains. Gardenias on the pillow or night blooming jasmine all add to an air of romance.

Some final thoughts on flower giving:

Get to know your florist. Stop in the shop and pick out what looks good. Discuss it ahead of time. Better yet, grow them yourself. Give meaning and thought to your choice. Relate the flower to an occasion: do you remember your wedding flowers, is her personality as rare as an orchid, what is her favorite color, did she just paint her entire apartment pale peach (if so, don't bring her bright red and yellow zinnias)? For the ultimate statement, replace the bouquet once a week with a fresh bunch just as the old ones are dying. I guarantee, you will always be on her mind.

Candy

First of all, have you noticed if your "someone special" even eats candy, or is she constantly counting calories and working out six hours a day at the gym? If that's the case, candy is the <u>last</u> thing she wants. Assuming she does indulge in sweets, buy with Rule #4 in mind: buy quality. Does she have a favorite? Jelly beans, Hershey Kisses, gumdrops? In this case, quantity is effective. Buy

Chapter 2: Old Stand-Bys

several pounds and put them in a fun container such as a fish bowl, apothecary jar, or fine crystal bowl.

*C*hocolate has been the traditional gift of love and is often thought of as an aphrodisiac. Some scientists believe that chocolate is a sex substitute because every 100 grams of it contains up to 660 milligrams of phenyl ethylamine, a stimulant closely related to the body's own dopamine and adrenaline. By raising blood pressure, heart rate, glucose levels and heightening sensations, this chemical induces a high similar-in-kind to a sexual climax. Other scientists say it is psychology, not chemistry, that gives chocolate its appeal. Whether real or perceived, for many, chocolate brings on a euphoria similar to the feeling of falling in love.

*I*t is estimated that Americans consume approximately 1.8 billion pounds of chocolate a year, costing $3 billion annually. We spend about $665 million alone on candy each Valentine's Day, much of it for boxed chocolate. Thanks in part to the Internet, your choices have been expanded to anywhere in the country. *Consumer Reports* sampled 19 companies this year. The top three choices came from lesser-known makers. Their experts looked for smooth, even-melting, chocolaty chocolate; fillings that tasted of real cream, butter, and vanilla; and fresh-tasting, easily identifiable nuts and fruits or fruit preserves.

Gifts Guaranteed to Please a Woman

- **Martine's**

$54 for one pound; found in Bloomingdale's department store in New York.

- **La Maison du Chocolat Coffret Maison**

$72 for 20 ounces; has two New York shops.

- **Candinas**

Thirty-six-piece box $41 for one pound sells only from its factory in Verona, Wisconsin.

If you enjoy traditional fillings and want to spend a bit less, consider the following very good one-pound boxes: Bernard Callebaut Copper Box Assortment, $36, Godiva Chocolatier Gold Ballotin, $33.

So save the Whitman Samplers you might buy at Walgreen's for the postman. Instead, spring for the best Belgian, Swiss, or French chocolates, even if you could only afford a very small box. Think of all the sensual ways you can put this gift to use. An exciting way to finish a romantic meal is to French Kiss with an after dinner mint. A perfect way to finish the perfect evening is to paint each other with chocolate body paint and enjoy licking it off. You might as well forget the calories and add the whip cream. Bon Appetit!

Chapter 2: Old Stand-Bys

Jewelry

- **Diamonds**

Let's talk about a girl's basic jewelry wardrobe. Starting with diamonds of course. Marilyn Monroe sang it in *"How to Marry a Millionaire"* - "Diamonds are a girl's best friend". (Although that turn of phrase probably originated in the marketing department of the DeBeers diamond cartel.) Yes, diamonds go with everything and if you can afford one, go for it. An exception is for a woman of the anti-materialistic-socialistic bend. If that's the case, she probably thinks all jewelry is garish and in bad taste. Remember to buy the best you can afford from a reputable dealer. Make sure the person you are buying from is a graduate gemologist and has been in business longer than the local Taco Bell. Diamonds are rated in four categories:

Gifts Guaranteed to Please a Woman

Cut: not to be confused with shape, but refers to the way the facets or flat surfaces are angled. The ideal cut offers more brilliance.

Clarity: the fewer imperfections or inclusions, the better.

Carat: weight, the larger the diamond usually indicates it is more rare

Color: close to no color is the rarest

𝒟on't be fooled just by size. No woman wants what the industry calls a "spready stone" or "matzos". That's a big, flat stone with an imperfection so big you can see it with the naked eye. Other no-nos are: don't buy single cut-diamond chips or small diamonds overwhelmed in a big setting... as if you were going to pass it off for 50 carats. If you are trying to surprise her with an engagement ring, a lot of subtle research is important. What kind of shape does she want: brilliant  (round), emerald (rectangular), square, marquis, oval, pear or heart?

Chapter 2: Old Stand-Bys

You get more weight for the money with the brilliant cut. The others cost about 30 percent more for the same weight measured in carats.

*I*n choosing a setting, you should consider whether she likes yellow gold, white gold, or platinum (even whiter than white gold). Many jewelers will suggest the actual diamond be set with prongs in white gold so it won't cast any yellow onto the diamond but the band, can be yellow gold if she prefers. Would your fiancée choose the classic solitaire or something more elaborate? Is her style contemporary or antique? Some secret talks with her girlfriends or mother may give some insight. Don't forget the option of fine antique or estate rings. The classic approach includes 3-stone rings in platinum or yellow gold. Alternatively, platinum filigree mountings with lovely old European diamonds, give the sense of a long history of love.

*A*fter she has her basic engagement and wedding rings, a guard ring is a nice addition. Sometimes given to mark the birth of a child or anniversary, these narrow bands of gold or platinum (often set with diamonds, sapphires or rubies) are worn in addition to the other rings.

• Gold

Moving onto gold. Again, buy only the best: 18 karat not 14 karat, not 10 karat, not gold-filled nor electro-plated. No matter how small, buy the best quality. There are 24 parts to pure gold but that is too soft to use for jewelry so alloys are added to make it durable. Jewelry is a hard gift to return (she would not want to hurt your feelings), so consider the person you are trying to please. Notice what she already wears and why she likes it. If she never wears a necklace or pin, don't start her collection now. When you are out shopping, pass by a jewelry store window. Almost all women will offer a comment about what they find attractive (not that she's dropping a hint or anything)! *Tiffany's* sends out a nice catalog, which could be conveniently hidden in a pile of mail to open a discussion. Starting at the top, earrings. Does she wear pierced or clip-on? Does she prefer tiny, dainty, or large cauliflower size? Have you seen her wear a drop earring - those that have something hanging from the earlobe? If she doesn't have tons of fine jewelry, stay with something basic that she can wear a lot and people won't say, "Oh, you have those bumble bee earrings on again".

• Silver

Sterling silver is an alternative when gold is too expensive or your lady just prefers the color. Make sure it is solid sterling silver. It must be stamped "sterling" if manufactured in the United States. Don't buy silver-plated jewelry . . . that is way too tacky!

Chapter *2*: Old Stand-Bys

- **Pearls**

Pearls are a basic part of any jewelry wardrobe. Pearls traditionally were symbols of virtue, chastity, wisdom and purity. As with diamonds, pearls are judged and priced according to standards of size, luster, shape and color. Various types include natural sometimes called oriental. These are the most expensive because they are found naturally when a grain of sand or other irritant finds its way into the shell of a giant oyster. With cultured pearls, the irritant is not natural, it is added by man.

Size: measured in millimeters

Luster: mirror-like finish, clean of imperfections. Surface shine gives pearls glowing beauty.

Shape: round, baroque, etc. How well matched is one to the other on a strand in all the above categories. Perfectly round are most rare and therefore most expensive.

Color: ranges from pink - silver - cream, white, gold-green, and shades of gray to black.

Gifts Guaranteed to Please a Woman

The length depends on the size of the woman. Pearls come in three basic lengths: Choker - 18", Matinee - 24" and Opera - 30". If she is petite, she is going to look like a flapper in a 30" Opera length. If she is a large woman, an 18" choker will literally choke her. Stick with something in the middle. Pearls are so versatile that they are a classic piece of jewelry and can be worn with everything from jeans to evening gowns. A beautiful diamond clasp can make the necklace more unique. **Simulated Pearls – forget it - no fakes please!**

- **Watches**

Think of the lines you can use on the gift card. "You are on my mind all the time." "I mark the hours 'til we are together". "For the time of your life." "I love spending time with you." When choosing a watch, consider her life-style. If she is a jock, she probably doesn't need a gold dress watch. Some great sport watch will do such as Breitling, Swiss Army, or TAG-Heuer. Techno Marine is especially hot now.

For fun and less expensive suggestions, visit a watch station at your local mall. This chain offers trendy watches by many manufacturers or click on www.sunglasshut.com (they own Watch Station). They are what they are and don't pretend to be anything else. Prices range from $50 to $400. If you can afford the fine classic solid gold watch, go for it. This means an 18-karat solid gold case, not gold filled. Adding a big gold band adds an extra-big price tag.

Chapter 2: Old Stand-Bys

Alligator or leather bands are perfectly acceptable. A step up is Rolex, Cartier, Chopard, Tiffany, Baume & Mercier, Jaeger-Le Coultre, from $2,000 - $100,000.

𝒟ress watches are for the girl who has everything and attends black tie affairs no less than five times a week. In the antique categories: 1920s platinum, black ribbon or cord band with diamonds around the face and band are delicate and fine in all price ranges; 1940s cocktail watches in pink and/or yellow gold with or without diamonds or colored stones have a more bracelet look, retro watches are available in all price ranges. If you want to second-mortgage your home, some contemporary dress watch suggestions are: Patek Phillipe, Cartier, Chopard, and Bulgari from $5,000 - $50,000 and up.

𝒮o whatever baubles, bangles and bright shiny things you give to your love, know they will be treasured and passed down the family tree.

Perfumes

𝒲omen have been using scents since the beginning of time to enhance their sex appeal. Here's a little history to help you understand why perfume is a classic gift. When Cleopatra prepared to receive Anthony aboard her barge, the sails would have been drenched with cyprium. The canopy above her seat, was garlanded with fragrant roses. After the bath, the rich Egyptian woman would lie naked

Gifts Guaranteed to Please a Woman

while her slave girls massaged fragrant oils and ointments into her skin. Cleopatra was one of the most famous fragrance-worshipers and probably inspired the Greeks and Romans to become sophisticated fragrance devotees as well.

The Romans were obsessed with the rose. Rosewater perfumed their public baths and flowed from fountains in the emperors' palaces.

Chapter *2*: Old Stand-Bys

Wine was rose-scented. At banquets and feasts, roses were strewn everywhere; even the cushions were stuffed with petals. If you needed a love potion it would, of course, taste of roses. Nero always slept on a bed of rose petals. At certain lavish banquets, a covey of white doves, whose wings had been impregnated with perfumes, was released to permeate the atmosphere. Josephine delighted in the scent of musk and violets. When she died in 1814, Napoleon had her grave covered with violet plants.

Queen Elizabeth I lived in a "bathless age". The use of soap was infrequent. Perfumes helped make life bearable. The relationship between perfume and fashion grew with the perfumed glove. In the thirteenth century, a lady's glove was given to a gentleman as a symbol of love. Because the curing process of the leather glove left a bad odor, perfumed oils from Grass, France were used to soften and scent.

*F*ragrance appears to be one of the original secrets of nature. Throughout the animal kingdom, scent plays an important part in courtship and in mating. Many species of animals are known to possess substances called pheromones whose scent triggers the lust of the opposite sex. You probably know this if you've ever been around a female dog in heat. Do human males and females carry pheromones? The question cannot yet be answered. But certainly, scent plays a part in human love even if on an unconscious level. When we kiss, we are performing a ceremony of greeting by smelling. In many primitive languages, the word for "kiss" or

- *29* -

"greet" is the same as that for "smell". Scientific studies show that a woman's hormonal scent should not be masked with too much cover up. Sexual arousal is linked with this subliminal scent.

Fragrance acts as an invisible "influence". With names like *Poison* and *Obsession*, we get an idea of what they are supposed to do. Scientists believe that the brain's complex system for cataloging and identifying smells is closely linked to other areas involved in the storage of memories. Smells, memories, and emotions are all inexorably linked. Fragrances can stir memories or create them. So what memories do you want to create? The *Fragrance Foundation* divides fragrances into categories to help guide in the selection process:

I. *Exhilarating/Energetic*

- **Green**

Usually the top note of a fragrance composition denotes the zest and energy of freshly cut grass and dewy-green leaves. Creates a young, vigorous mood in a fragrance. Examples include: *Calyx* by Perscriptives, Relaxing Fragrances by Shiseido, *Cristalle* by Chanel.

- **Spicy**

Connotes fragrances that obtain their notes from several sources; actual spices such as cinnamon, cloves, ginger, and cardamom; and flowers that possess traces of spicy notes such as carnation and lavender. Examples include: *Coco* by Chanel, *Tabu* by Dana, *Opium* by Yves Saint Laurent.

- **Woodsy Mossy**

Fragrances containing unmistakably clean, clear crispness. Sandalwood, rosewood, cedar, and other aromatic woods are combined with earthy oak moss and fern to create scents refreshingly "foresty". Examples include: *Must* by Cartier, *Knowing* by Esteé Lauder, *Fendi* by Fendi.

II. *Relaxing/Understated*

- ### Single Floral

A single floral captures the scent of a single flower such as a rose, carnation, violet or lilac. Examples include: *Gardénia Passion* by Annick Goutal, *Michael* by Michael Kors.

- ### Fruity

Fruity blends are recognized by either a clean, fresh citrus quality of oranges and lemons or by smooth, mellow peach-like warmth. Examples include: *Eau d'Hadrien* by Annick Goutal, *Au Thé Vert* by Bulgari, *Polo Sport Woman* by Ralph Lauren.

III. *Romantic/Poetic*

- ### Floral Bouquet

An intricately blended bouquet of individual flower notes which are given balance and body by a combination of base notes including woods, greens, ambers, etc. Examples include: *Allure* by Chanel, *Joy* by Jean Patou, *J'adore* by Christain Dior, *Kenzo* by Kenzo.

IV. *Erotic/Mysterious*

• **Oriental Blend**

*S*ophisticated and sultry, this uninhibited fragrance type is achieved through a blending of brilliant exotic flowers, herbs and fixatives. It is designed to have a strong, erotic appeal. Examples include: *Hanae Mori* by Hanae Mori, *Shalimar* by Guerlain, *Obsession* by Calvin Klein.

*T*here are two other categories that you hear a lot about. The first is unisex, worn by both men and women. They include: *Declaration* by Cartier, *CK One* by Calvin Klein, *Merge* by Xankim. The other popular category is relaxation. Products include items for the bath, massage and aromatherapy. Fragrances such as *Zen* by Shiseido and *Aroma Calm* by Lancôme are good examples. Check out health and beauty stores found in your local shopping mall or on the web, such as: *Aveda Environmental Lifestyle Store, Bath & Body Shop Works, I. Natural, Sephora* and *The Body Shop.*

*I*f the woman in your life is young, let's say college age, she may be a little more experimental since she hasn't had time to try everything under the sun. By the time a woman is 30 or 40, she has tried a lot of scents and knows exactly what she likes. Many a bottle of Chanel No. 5 has gone back to the store or been sold at a tag sale. If you are going to experiment with something new, try to stay in the basic category. Check out the brands she presently uses.

Sometimes she wears one type at work and another type for evening, or changes from a lighter scent in the summer to a heavier one in the winter. Take these names to a good perfumery (a store that sells only perfume and can show you similar scents in the same family). Purchasing perfume from a cosmetic counter in a department store is limiting. The sales help won't know about other fragrances nor do they make a commission on anything but their own brands.

Fragrances can be found in different forms.

- **Perfume**

Perfume is the strongest, longest-lasting fragrance form. Like lipstick, blusher or eye make-up, it provides the intensity and the emphasis. Apply at all the pulse points - where one feels the beat of the heart. Fragrance rises, and properly applied will heighten the application. The heat of the body at these points will intensify the perfume's impact.

- **Eau de Parfum**

One of the newest forms of fragrances to be found in many of the fine fragrance collections, it assures a long lasting concentrated application and prepares the skin for the perfume application. It should be smoothed or sprayed, just before dressing, all over the body from the feet up.

Chapter 2: Old Stand-Bys

- **Eau de Toilette**

Usually less concentrated than eau de perfume, it also provides the foundation for your perfume application and should be applied in exactly the same way as eau de perfume.

- **Cologne**

Cologne is the lightest form of fragrance. Perfect for splashing liberally all over the body. It is the perfect refresher. It does not provide a longer lasting fragrance application.

Don't buy the jumbo industrial size bottle no matter how impressive it may appear. Perfume changes over time from the effects of light and heat. Most women don't store it in an optimum environment of cool and dark. Therefore once opened, it is perishable.

You might want to get her the lotion, soap, bubble bath, or powder that goes with her favorite scent. A purse size is also a good idea. Sprays are a good idea because they don't contaminate the original container with body oils from the applicator. On the other hand, those elegant crystal perfume bottles look so good on the dressing table.

A girlfriend told me about a man who waited until his wife was on a phone call with her family. He then lined a pathway into the bathroom with scented candles, drew a bath with scented bath salts, and called her upstairs. When she was in the tub, he presented her

Gifts Guaranteed to Please a Woman

with a collection of wonderful bath and beauty products on a silver tray. What a romantic presentation.

What if you love her but hate the scent she wears? If you think you can get her to try a new fragrance, great. If you can tell her without hurting her feelings, that's terrific. If this is too tough, develop an allergy. A good sneezing fit should do it. Another option is to tell her what really turns you on is soap and water. This is true for many men who just like the smell of a woman right out of the shower. Maybe a little baby oil and powder.

Chapter 2: Old Stand-Bys

The fragrance you chose should personify the intangible qualities that make her unique. If you are lucky, maybe you can apply it to her pulse points: behind the ears, inside the wrists, at the temples, at the base of her throat, at the bosom, and even behind the knees and inside the ankles. As the sun goes down and the evening heats up, you can follow the scent in the dark.

Cards

Hallmark has come a long way. With categories in the inspirational, motivational, miss you, romantic, thinking of you, I appreciate you, friendship, love, and new love, they have covered almost all the bases. The best cards are still home made. OK, cheat a little and get some ideas from store bought cards. If you can't draw, use cut out images from magazines. Crayon and childlike drawings will melt the hardest heart. It shows your vulnerabilities and a romantic, creative side she may not have known you had.

𝓑lank cards, without a pre-printed message, give you an opportunity to be creative and say something personal that only she will understand. Win her over with humor. If you can make her laugh you're ahead of the game. I love Gary Larson's *Farside* cards. He gives human qualities to animals that point to the absurdity of our lifestyle.

𝓢exually explicit cards can be funny, a "turn on", or insulting, depending on your partner. Let's assume you know when and if it would be appropriate to send her one of these. Maybe you should sign it from a secret admirer and see if she mentions it. If she doesn't, you know you have competition.

Lingerie

𝓦hile a great opportunity to explore your sexual fantasy, this gift presents a bit of a challenge. Where Robert may have fantasies of black leather crotch-less panties and 4-inch spike heels from *Frederick's of Hollywood*, his wife, Susan, prefers her two-piece flannel pajamas. Let's talk about mainstream options for the moment. Lingerie is an intimate luxury every woman loves. Go to the best store you can afford. Buy something she will be comfortable wearing. If she is self-conscious about her wide hips, don't buy her a microscopic G-string. If she is small breasted and worries about it, don't buy her a Wonder Bra to remind her you are also concerned. A beautiful silk gown is a good solution in both

Chapter *2*: Old Stand-Bys

cases. Check to be sure the item can be returned. Many stores only allow a credit.

Lingerie Lingo

- **Teddy**

Short unstructured one-piece garment, usually silk, like a mini slip with divided leg.

- **Tap Pants**

Full cut wide leg panties, usually silk or silk/satin. They are similar to the pants worn by dancers in musicals of the 1930s and 1940s.

- **Merry Widow**

Tight-fitting, one-piece undergarment with built-in bra and garter belt.

- **Bustier**

Cinched upper garment, with built-in bra, worn with or without an outer garment.

Bras and panties are a little harder to fit. If you don't know her size, look on the label (when she is not wearing them, of course). Garter belts and stockings are fun, but I know lots of women who feel too self-conscious to wear them, even in the bedroom. It's worth a try. Be sure you can return them if she absolutely refuses to wear them. If tacky underwear turns you on, maybe this is the exception to buying quality. In fact, maybe the cheaper the better. Have fun and experiment with this category.

Chapter 2: Old Stand-Bys

*D*on't go too far out on a limb. Sarah was horrified when her husband John bought her a brown, fake fur robe that he thought was "cuddly". She felt like a gorilla when she put it on but wore it the entire winter feeling like King Kong.

Gifts Guaranteed to Please a Woman

Chapter 3

Original Creations

Make a Film

*V*ideo is an inexpensive way to mark a special occasion. It also gives you an opportunity to impress her with your skills as a director. An example: for her birthday, film each of her best friends giving her a birthday wish. It was a great success as the feature attraction at a surprise party I attended. Each friend was filmed for one to two minutes. Don't let them go on and on. It gets boring. Practice it a few times if they need to, then do it in one "take", otherwise, you have a lot of editing. A more elaborate version with voiceovers and music overlays can be done, but this runs into money for a professional editing studio. There is software available for those of you who are computer savvy. Some were sincere, some sang a song, some wrote and recited a poem, while others got together complete with props and acted out a funny skit roasting the birthday honoree. Of course, you should be filmed last. Complete the feature with a title card at the beginning and credits at the end, drawn on cardboard with magic marker lettering. If you are in a hurry, just make a simple tape of your feelings, filmed on location. Pick a spot that means something to both of you: the beach where you met, in front of your favorite restaurant, some place you will identify with. Write down reasons you are in love with her or read poetry written by the pros…now, once more with feeling! I guarantee, this is something she will cherish. If you don't have time to do these projects, at least you could rent a romantic video to share over a bowl of popcorn. Remember, <u>you</u> bring the popcorn, candy, etc. Movie suggestions are: *An Affair to Remember*, *Sleepless in Seattle* (both great "chick flicks"). Also try *While you were Sleeping*, *Gone with the Wind*, or *Sabrina* (the original with Audrey Hepburn).

Chapter 3: Original Creations

Make an Album

Compile photographs you have taken over the past year or since the beginning of your relationship. This is a very thoughtful gift she will love. Write the date and place on the back of the photos for future reference. Buy a nice leather album with acid-free paper so the photos will not chemically change color over time. Frame the best shot of the two of you. If you don't have a great one, give her a portrait session with a good portrait photographer . . . not the guy at Kmart with the blue velvet back drop. Make a scrap book containing photos, the menu or wine list from your favorite restaurant, souvenirs from trips or outings, snippets of poems, or quotable quotes. Show her that your shared history, however brief or long it may be, means as much to you as it does to her.

The written word: Use your writing skills

- **The love letter**

Write your feelings for her. Tell her what she means to you, how much joy she brings to your life. Describe something she does that turns you on. What do you find most beautiful about her? Women *never* get tired of hearing these things, and your letter is something she can get out on a lonely night when you are out of town and read over and over and over. Better yet, tape your love letter so she can hear the feeling in your voice.

Gifts Guaranteed to Please a Woman

- **A poem**

What's your style - iambic pentameter, haiku or just plain limerick? Even if it's corny, you get points for effort. This of course should be read to her with full expression. If you can't compose something, buy it. A book of Lord Byron's sonnets is an old favorite. Other romantic standbys include anything by Shelley, Browning, and Keats. Remember to sign and date the inside front cover. Include a sterling silver bookmark to note a special passage. Good contemporary choices are, *Poems of Love Forever* by Cealozo, *Cupid's Arrow*, *Love Poems* by Sommer, *From the Heart* by Shaw. An anthology, like *A Book of Love Poetry* edited by Jon Stallworthy, has a sampling of every famous poet.

Chapter *3*: Original Creations

- **A simple note**

A love note in her purse, briefcase or suitcase costs nothing but carries a lot of weight. Refrigerator, bathroom mirror and steering wheel are also posting places. Say you've been together for a meeting, a lunch, an overnight tryst. When she's not looking, hide a note where she will find it later. Tell her, if nothing else, you love her . . . are thinking about her. For the more imaginative, be more specific, "I miss your sweet smell", "I want to run my fingers through your long, silky hair." Important: make sure it's put in a place where it doesn't fall out at a business meeting and embarrass her.

Gifts Guaranteed to Please a Woman

Painting

*I*f you have talent in this area, artwork is a wonderful way of communicating your love. Share with her your vision of something she cares about: a special place you've visited, a sketch of her dog, her garden. Be careful about a portrait of her unless you can guarantee a flattering rendition.

Say it with Music

*S*ing a song, play an instrument. You may not be Rogers and Hammerstein, but if you have any musical talent, compose and/or sing a song. Change the lyrics to an old favorite tune or just sing her favorite song. One of my best memories is having a toast sung to me at my birthday party. If your singing voice is more punishment than pleasure and you can't play an instrument, then buy your musical expression. There are plenty of love songs, old and new, to send her the message.

Chapter 3: Original Creations

For the more technologically minded, mix and burn a CD of special and meaningful songs that express your feelings about her.

Things that Grow

Give a living gift, something that grows and blossoms like your love. Plant a tree, some flowers, a whole garden, depending on your green thumb. Bulbs are great because they come up every year and multiply. I know a man who planted a flowering fruit tree every year on his wife's birthday. After a few years, she had an orchard and they could eat the succulent fruit. If you don't have the time or talent to plant it, hire a gardener.

Gifts Guaranteed to Please a Woman

Chapter 4: Special Events

Chapter *4*

Special Events

Birthdays

This is a big day. You bought her a big house in the best neighborhood, now you can sit back and forget her birthday? It's only one day. What's the big deal? BIG FAUX PAS... NEVER... FORGET ABOUT IT! It's the little things that count to a woman. Start the celebration early with breakfast in bed or a balloon bouquet in the closet or bathroom. Even though she says she is getting older and doesn't want to be reminded, ignore her comments and proceed with the celebration. Cook a romantic dinner for two. Have it catered if you are a klutz in the kitchen. If this idea doesn't appeal to you, make dinner reservations at her favorite restaurant. I knew a man who always double-booked restaurants to give her a choice. Remember to cancel the one she doesn't choose. Go the day before to pick out the most private corner table. Meet the maitre d'. Find out if he will be there the night of her birthday to assure all the finishing touches will be taken care of. Special attention requires a New York handshake – as you know that's a $20 bill passed to him

Gifts Guaranteed to Please a Woman

discreetly. Arrange for special flowers at the table, and don't forget the cake. Some restaurants allow you to bring your own. Others prefer their chef make it. Maybe you just arrange for her favorite dessert with a candle. After dessert, give her the present. If it is too big to be opened at the table, go back to your place where you can enjoy it privately. If you, or the birthday girl, find a group of singing waiters offensive, pass on it. Just whisper "Happy birthday, I love you". That's all that need be said.

How about the party, especially on the milestone birthdays - 30, 40, and 50? Is she the type of woman who enjoys the attention or would she simply die of embarrassment? One poor husband with the best of intentions started planning a surprise 50th birthday celebration for his wife one year in advance. His guest list included

Chapter 4: Special Events

hundreds of people from the past including a ballet teacher from grade school. Guests from around the US and Europe were going to be included with celebrities sending videotaped messages. A complete hotel was to be rented, full orchestra, formal sit down dinner, shuttle service - you get the picture. Unfortunately or fortunately, as the case may be, his wife found out before the invitations were sent. She went ballistic. No way did she want a party for her 50th. Too much! Too embarrassing! Instead, a month before her birthday, a girlfriend talked her into an overnight pajama party at a great hotel in New York with ten of her closest friends in attendance. They were given the task of bringing a gift they had created. The gifts became the entertainment after dinner. She was comfortable with this and had a great time. The actual day of her birthday, she spent celebrating with her husband at their vacation home, just the two of them.

If in doubt, ask her opinion. Tell her you would like to ask two other couples, ten of her friends, rent a private room for 50, charter a yacht, set up a tent for 100, whatever you have in mind and can afford. However it ends up, you get the credit and appreciation from her for thinking of the idea and following up on the execution. After any dinner party, don't forget the toast (and I don't mean the bread and butter kind.) Prepare this ahead of time. Make it good and from the heart. If you don't have a clue as to what she wants, ask her questions about the best and worst presents she ever received. Give her a questionnaire about favorite music, flowers, color, foods, etc. You should be able to come up with the perfect something with this additional information.

- **The Cake**

Homemade is always a nice gesture. If you don't feel like an accomplished pastry chef, purchasing one is okay, but find a good bakery. Don't stop off at the local supermarket and pick up a $4.99 special with icing made from lard. Don't buy chocolate because it's your favorite. What is her favorite? Order this cake ahead of time so they can write a message on the top in the icing. Search out a pastry chef who specializes in spun sugar creations that can be made (at a price) to look like whatever your heart imagines. What if she doesn't eat cake? Be creative. Buy a large fruit tart, cherry pie, or frozen soufflé. What if she is on a strict diet: no sugar, no calories? Try a large gelatin mold using diet Jell-O. What if she is a health nut? Ask the baker for the local health food store to do a carrot cake with whole-wheat flour, rice syrup or honey for sweetener. They know what to put in it. The point is, be considerate of her preferences. If she is over 25, you may need a blowtorch to light all the candles. Instead, use single digit candles, a "2" and a "5" for example. One candle serves the purpose of making a wish. Always sing happy birthday when you are in a private setting. It's optional if you think it's inappropriate in a public place.

Chapter *4*: Special Events

Anniversary

*L*ike the ad says, "Tell her you would do it all over again". I think that slogan is meant to sell a diamond eternity ring (a continuous band of diamonds). Not a bad idea, if you can afford it. Some other thoughts are to revisit your honeymoon. Or, take the honeymoon you never had. For example, let's take Paris as a destination. Fill a big basket with French champagne, tickets to a designer fashion show, paté, French bread, perfume, plane tickets and a brochure of the hotel. She will be dazzled. This same get-a-way can be done simply and inexpensively to a country retreat. Just package and arrange it with the same attention to detail. Some couples who renew their vows even have another ceremony. Just don't let the

Gifts Guaranteed to Please a Woman

date go unnoticed. A homemade card is better than nothing. Give something to honor each year. For a 15th anniversary, how about 15 golden candles, 15 diamonds on a necklace, 15 shares of a Blue Chip stock, 15 of her favorite flowers, 15 acres of prime seafront property to build that future vacation home. Give something the two of you can share throughout the year. Create a calendar with the anniversary date marked on each month with a date for dinner.

Remember how she begged you to dance with her at your brother's wedding? Give her a gift certificate for ballroom dancing lessons. This sincere effort on your part will be greatly appreciated. You might not become another Fred Astaire, but you may actually enjoy it. If she likes classical music, a series of symphony tickets is a great gift. Make sure they are good seats, not the nosebleed section in the upper, upper balcony.

Chapter 4: Special Events

Christmas/Hanukkah (and other miscellaneous holidays)

If it's a family affair, be sure you arrive early to help. Don't arrive with the guests after the house has been cleaned and decorated, gifts for the entire family purchased and wrapped, menu planned and prepared. Somewhere along the line, some men have the false impression their only job is to grace us with their presence on these occasions and maybe open a bottle of wine or carve the turkey. Not good enough. After the big family dinner, do you watch the football games with the rest of the couch potatoes? Even if you hate doing dishes, at least keep her company while she washes the crystal by hand and polishes the silver. Better yet, offer to help, but learn how to do it right. Don't chip the china plates and drop a few glasses to show how inept you are. Be aware of the emotional pressure that comes with the holiday season. It's during this time when expectations are the greatest and disappointment keenest. Find a romantic time for the two of you before the guests arrive or after the kids have written Santa's note and are tucked in bed. The material gifts can be easily wrapped and put under the tree, but time is the most precious gift you can give during Christmas or anytime.

Gifts Guaranteed to Please a Woman

Mother's Day

*E*ven though she is not <u>your</u> mother, remind her children how important this day is and give them suggestions. If you are the father of her children, why not recognize her for being a caring mother. A guard ring for each child is a great idea. A guard ring consists of narrow bands that go around the wedding ring, usually set with small precious stones. A trophy with the engraving "World's Best Mom" wouldn't hurt. A photo album made by the kids with their favorite shots of their mother will bring tears to her eyes, but usually requires your help. Now is when you should be CEO of the family and oversee the children's Mother's Day gift project. What if you all make a little book with each page having a poem about mothers, a picture drawn by one of the children and, most importantly, each of you giving the reason she is the World's Best Mom.

Valentine's Day

*V*alentine's Day is a day for lovers. While you may not understand why it's so, love and romance will always be the most important aspect of the relationship to her, <u>always</u>. This is where we separate the men from the girls. You <u>can't</u> be <u>too</u> romantic on Valentine's Day. Let her know you think she is the sexiest female in the world. How do you express this passion? There are the old stand-bys (see

Chapter 4: Special Events

Chapter 2 on Flowers, Jewelry and Candy). There is nothing wrong with any of them. How about a combination care package? It's fun opening up a lot of little gifts. If she is uninhibited and experimental, consider these possibilities. Lacy, red, crotch-less panties (tell her they are just a joke even though you hope she will try them), matching garter belt, stockings, cherry flavored love oil, red condoms, erotic valentine card, chocolate in the shape of lips or an exotic video. These items can be purchased from those X-rated novelty shops (you wouldn't be caught dead in) or on the web. All items should be wrapped individually in red tissue or valentine paper and sprinkled with small, red, metallic hearts (purchased at a card store) before closing the entire box. Finish with a big satin bow. Careful! Know your Valentine! This could be insulting to some women. If she would be embarrassed by this erotic assortment, the care package can be modified to include a red, silk teddy, slip, perfume with names like Passion or Obsession, an old fashioned valentine card, a chocolate rose

Gifts Guaranteed to Please a Woman

or a big Hershey's kiss, a coffee mug with sayings like "Please Be Mine". (These can be found at stationary and candy stores). A stuffed teddy bear is too, too cute but what the heck, it's Valentine's Day! How about a treasure hunt with clues on small children's Valentine cards with you as the treasure. If you've done everything right, it will be a memorable night of fun, romance, and passion. Good Luck!

Job Well Done

Make your own special occasion. Reward her for a job well done.

- She loses 30-pounds and meets her diet goal. Take her out and buy her a new dress. Go with her to watch her try on clothes. <u>Don't get visibly bored</u>. Lavish her with compliments on everything she tries on.

- She finishes her Spanish course with an 'A'. Okay, so you don't have to take her to Spain, but how about a Spanish restaurant where she can demonstrate her skills.

- She gets a promotion at work. A new briefcase, laptop computer, *Palm Pilot* or *Filofax* may be in order.

- She runs her first mini-marathon but doesn't finish in the top 100. So what! Buy her your own 1st Place ribbon or

Chapter 4: Special Events

trophy with her name engraved. Most sporting good stores or engraving shops sell these. Let her know she is #1 in your eyes.

- She gets her real estate license and/or sells her first house. A sterling silver key chain is an appropriate prize.

Gifts Guaranteed to Please a Woman

- She closes a big contract with XYZ Corporation. Give her a *Mont Blanc* pen with which to sign all those future contracts.

- She gets tenure at an ivy league college. Give her that hard-to-find signed, limited edition, leather-bound book by her favorite author.

- She gets her first part in a major film, play, etc. A designer evening bag with theater tickets would be fun to celebrate her accomplishment.

Chapter 5: The Gift of an Experience

Chapter 5

The Gift of an Experience

Trip Fantastic

A gift of a great escape is fabulous! This is a time for the two of you to relax and enjoy each other without the kids, the hectic schedules. Things to remember when giving a vacation: be sure it's something <u>she</u> would like. We know <u>you</u> have always wanted to go salmon fishing and camp along the Snake River, but is that her idea of a good time? Plan ahead to give her an opportunity without jeopardizing her schedule. Be flexible.

Gifts Guaranteed to Please a Woman

*I*f children are involved, have you made arrangements with a relative or someone she trusts to take care of the kids? Of course, most women feel guilty leaving their children on important days such as birthdays, first day of school, recitals. Plan around this. Take her away as "First Class" as you can afford; better a weekend at *The Plaza* in New York with a limo than a two-week stay at the *Holiday Inn* in Atlantic City. Maybe it's just a day's drive to a romantic hotel on the seacoast. It can still be memorable if you take care of details. This means transportation, food, flowers, and activities. If this is your new lover, don't say you want her to join you for a romantic dinner in the city without providing the transportation. Make reservations at restaurants ahead of time or stock food for a vacation home. The last thing she wants to do is shop and cook just like she does at home. Speaking from experience, I remember all the trips to my "vacation" home in Florida where I did nothing but shop, cook, do the laundry, and clean up wet swimming suits and towels dropped on the bed and floor. I kept saying to myself, "Am I having fun yet?"

*P*lan activities, do your research ahead of time. Know what show, plays, museums, attractions are available. You can get this information from your travel agent, Chamber of Commerce, internet or a key magazine found in the hotel (check with the concierge). Call a friend who loves and has visited your destination. Ask your secretary to help you work on it, but don't give a trip and make the

Chapter 5: The Gift of an Experience

recipient plan it. If you get there and decide to relax and never leave the room, great! At least you knew the options. Candles, flowers, and wine or champagne are always a nice touch waiting in the room. Maybe root beer is her favorite drink. Know it and have it waiting.

A recently divorced friend of mine told me about a weekend in the mountains of Colorado where her new beau found the perfect rustic log cabin (Ralph Lauren-style with 20-foot vaulted ceilings, massive stone fireplace, hot tub . . . you get the picture). He brought her favorite CDs and prepared an incredible meal. Throughout dinner they talked about her favorite topics of poetry and politics. They shared a night of incredible sex (he also did research in this area). The next morning, they went cross-country skiing. He thought to have the skis rented and packed a picnic lunch complete with wine, cheese, and a blanket. She did nothing but enjoy. What a snow job!

Other Tips for Planning a Trip

- Be on time!
- Don't make her drive 90 miles an hour to catch a plane.
- Don't ever cancel unless it is an act of God. "An important business meeting came up" is no excuse. Lie to your boss, but don't cancel for business reasons.

Gifts Guaranteed to Please a Woman

- Don't bring that cellular phone that you normally have glued to your ear. If phone calls, faxes, or emails are necessary to keep your job, do it when she is occupied having a massage or taking a nap.

- If you are married, remember what it takes for a woman to leave her house, even for a weekend. Offer to help and, at the very least, acknowledge the amount of organizational skills she demonstrates. When a man leaves on a trip, he packs his suitcase (some don't even do that). When a woman leaves her house, she makes sure the wash is done, the house is clean, the food is cooked or arranged for, the plants are watered, the pets are cared for, and of course, the children's needs are all met - including a ride to the orthodontist and a car pool to the soccer game complete with the snack she promised to bring. Emergency numbers, back up help and itineraries are drilled into the baby-sitter, along with a list of plumbers, electricians, etc. should anything go wrong with the house. The newspapers, mail and bills have been attended to. Now, she can pack her suitcase.

Chapter 5: The Gift of an Experience

- The surprise trip is very effective but must have some parameters. She must be told in advance she is leaving to go somewhere for a specific number of days and what type of clothing to bring, i.e. dress casual for hot weather. Another option is to buy an entire new wardrobe when you get there but this could prove very expensive. You can also use the ruse of letting her think she is going to one place, like visiting her sister in Indiana and instead, changing the itinerary to the Vineyards of Sonoma Valley. This takes cooperation and collusion. Remember Rule #3, Presentation. Wrap hints about the destination in a map, cut the trip itinerary into a jigsaw puzzle, or send her on a treasure hunt around the house to find clues - with a ticket at the end. Give a gift of a suitcase with an appropriate new outfit to wear. A girlfriend of hers could help with this. Bon Voyage!

Mind Expanding

What are her passions? How does she spend her spare time? Gardening, flower arranging, art history, cooking, politics, dogs, ecology, painting, bird watching, investments? Maybe it's something she doesn't do but has always talked about learning. "Someday I'm going to learn French". Giving an educational gift of study is a great growth experience. There are so many courses offered from the inexpensive adult education at your local high school to the expensive, intensive one-on-one tutor. A Harvard MBA is not out of the question. It's up to you and what you can afford.

Think of the clever ways you can present this creative experience. Take for example, a course in flower arranging. First do your

Chapter 5: The Gift of an Experience

research: who is the flower guru in your area? Ask her friends. Ask the local garden club. You could present this with a collection of gifts - a new hand trowel, gardening gloves, pruning clippers, packages of seeds. Artfully arrange everything in a watering can or cutting basket with the class registration certificate tucked inside. Don't forget the bow. How about a cooking course? First, think about what type of food she most enjoys. Is her preference traditional French à la Julia Child? This presents possibilities as far reaching as the *Cordon Bleu* in Paris. What about Northern Italian? Oriental Wok cooking is also fun. Or possibly she is very health conscious and leans to vegetarian/spa cuisine. Go to a specialty store and ask for help, or call the instructor. Ask for suggestions they might have for the basic utensils needed for that particular style of cooking.

- *French cooking*: Package together in a big copper bowl: a whisk, *The Escoffier Cook Book* (a classic by the master chef), molds, champagne wine vinegar;

- *Oriental Cooking*: Package in a wok: chopsticks, bamboo steamer, strainer, soy sauce, oyster sauce, wasabi, cookbook;

- *Italian Cooking:* Package in a pasta bowl: olive oil, apron, cookbook, pastas, pesto sauce, wooden spoons, garlic head, or spices.

Gifts Guaranteed to Please a Woman

Soul Searching

*N*urture her spiritual and psychological side. Help her to explore the metaphysical realm. If she is religious, she might enjoy a retreat. Your priest, pastor, or rabbi can give you some suggestions. For peace and relaxation, a class in transcendental meditation or Tai chi could be interesting. If she doesn't have time for a class, *The Art of Happiness* by the Dalai Lama is a "mini course" in harmonious, daily living. Also, there are great relaxation tapes that transport you to a tropical beach for less than $10.

Chapter 5: The Gift of an Experience

If she believes in astrology, a psychic reading could be insightful and fun. You can supply key birth information to the astrologer and many will put it on tape so you can surprise her.

If you really want to help her to solve something that seriously bothers her emotionally, psychological counseling is an alternative. It would be wonderful to aid in her resolution of some conflict. Be prepared to get involved if you are part of the dynamics. Most family therapists do just that; they include the family. This is a caring and brave gift to give.

Body Improving

The gift of a healthy body is one of the best you can give. It shows her you really care about her welfare. The obvious jumpstart for this experience is a trip to a spa.

- Local day spas: massages, facials, manicures, pedicures
- Weekly spas: a more elaborate version of the day spa with exercise and a change of scenery
- Exercise class: personal trainer, active/passive yoga
- Sport lessons: tennis, skiing, golf
- Dancing lessons: jazz, tap, disco, ballroom

Gifts Guaranteed to Please a Woman

- Trip to the dermatologist for dermabrasion or *Botox* injections to soften those lines

- Plastic Surgery - okay, that's about the ultimate body-improving gift. (But hey, if she has hated her nose for 30 years and has talked about changing it, give her the support and the check to pay for it.)

Chapter 6

Sweet Nothings - Sensual Pleasures

Massage

For those who enjoy touching and being touched, give the gift of massage. If you do not naturally have those magic hands, there are books and courses to help. Don't worry. You won't have to know the difference between Swedish or Shiatsu. You could buy a series at the local spa but it's so much better to do it yourself. Why not give it a try. To present this, give her some yummy massage oils,

Gifts Guaranteed to Please a Woman

lavender for relaxation, eucalyptus for stimulation. I love the smell of almond oil. Aroma-therapy, which uses essential oils, is a very hot industry. Hundreds of essential oils can be used for different effects. The fun part is finding all her favorite places to be rubbed. My masseuse tells me a woman usually holds her stress in the back of the neck into the shoulders and sometimes the lower back. Don't rush this. Don't say your hands are tired. Don't turn wrestling mania on television. And *never push for sex after 10 minutes of rubbing.*

Find a quiet time; no phones. Play soft music. A good massage from head to toe lasts about one hour. While you are gently caressing her skin, whisper sweet nothings: "Your skin is so soft", "I love the back of your neck", or "Your toes are cute". Don't say "Ewww, that is one ugly scar". If she is not so relaxed that she falls asleep when you are finished, she may request a more intimate rubdown. Don't rush this, half the fun is getting there. Country singer Reba McEntire sang it best, "I want a lover with a slow hand."

Bubble Bath

Buy the most gorgeous bottle of bubble bath, bath salts or oils you can find or afford. Big is better; it looks great in the bathroom. Do not try to pass off that cheap junk from *Walgreens*. Good choices are: *Essential Elements, L'Occitane, Origins,* or *La Prairie.*

Chapter 6: Sweet Nothings – Sensual Pleasures

*S*mall scented votive candles are good to set the mood. If the tub is not big enough for both of you, she can soak while you massage her temples, hands or feet. Complete the occasion with champagne and music. Sometimes it is great just to celebrate the "Inner Child". This bathtub is set up for playtime with rubber duckies and toy boats, funny little soaps, and bubbles with wands to blow away the adult world.

Exotic Dancing

For the uninhibited, present yourself as her personal dancer for the evening, (complete with G-string). Most men will need a lot of alcohol as a primer. It's not for everyone, but if you have ever watched the afternoon talk shows when Oprah has the "Hunks from Chippendales" on, you will see the women go crazy - they make fools of themselves. Obviously, both people have to be comfortable with this little fantasy. If it works for you, put on the music and strut your stuff.

Up Close and Personal

Women have always been the caretakers of men, children, and each other. Why not turn the table and treat her to your own brand of TLC? Intimate gifts such as giving her a facial or brushing/washing her hair can be very sensual and caring gestures. Go to a good store and ask for help picking a facial cream or shampoo and conditioner. Read the instructions so you know how to apply it. This is a very loving gift and costs next to nothing.

Chapter *6*: Sweet Nothings – Sensual Pleasures

Love Slave

*N*o, I don't mean S&M with whips and chains. Try something new with your lover. Be her slave for the night. Explore her fantasies. Explicit books and movies may help stimulate ideas. Sexy lingerie, love oils and lubricants should open up a discussion anyway.

*D*o it in a new room - meet her in the garage as she comes home and relive the high school experience in the back seat. Surprise her when she is making dinner. See if you can get her mind off peeling carrots.

Gifts Guaranteed to Please a Woman

Hugs and Kisses

Give her coupons packaged in a pretty box or jar to be redeemed anytime for kisses, hugs, backrubs, or just time-out to talk. Give them a time value. Each is worth 5 minutes or whatever. When she presents them for redemption, honor them. Don't say you are too busy. That would be worse then not giving them at all.

The "I'm Sorry Gift"

You promised to take her away for a romantic weekend but you have to work instead. Send flowers with a note of apology for disappointing her.

Chapter 7

Manners Matter

*I*t's never too late to learn. If your parents didn't teach you, here are a few gifts of etiquette.

*N*ever, never talk on a cell phone while having dinner with your favorite lady. What phone call can't wait for an hour or two until you have finished eating? Unless your mother is on her deathbed (and in that case you should be at her side), what call can be that important?

Gifts Guaranteed to Please a Woman

If you are in the middle of a big business deal, at least turn off the phone at the table and check the messages when you go to the restroom.

A woman wants to think she has your undivided attention for this limited time.

Never arrive at a dinner party (even if she's cooking for just the two of you) without a hostess gift. This can be the traditional wine or flowers. Of course you get points for the more creative gift (such as take photos and send them later with your thank-you note). Obviously, if you are married and she cooks every night, this formality isn't necessary. That doesn't mean you can take her for granted – offer to help with the dishes; keep her company while she cooks; help prepare the meal together, or pick up dessert on the way home. It doesn't hurt to write a special thank you on her birthday and remind the children to thank her for all the yummy meals on Mother's Day.

Mothers teach your sons from an early age to acknowledge gifts given to them, whether tangible or acts of kindness. I was constantly impressed by a famous CEO of one of the largest companies in the world. He would always send a handwritten thank you in a timely manner, whether after a dinner party or a golf game. He even once responded back to a kind letter I sent him. I would always point this out to my son as an example of a very busy man who took the time

Chapter 7: Manners Matter

to recognize the thoughtfulness of others. This practice had to serve him well on his climb to the top. Obviously, his mother did a good job!

*N*ever forget a "thank you" for a gift. The gift could be one you open in a box or a thoughtful gesture (such as, she takes care of your sick dog while you are out of town). Say it, phone it, email, or write it.

*A*t a minimum, a verbal acknowledgement of her gift tells her you appreciate the thoughtfulness and you are not a selfish guy with an entitlement mentality. Phoning or emailing is better yet, and be sure to include details: "Thank you so much for my birthday dinner. I can't believe you went to all the trouble to get the recipe from my favorite Greek restaurant for Mousaka. It was better than I had in Athens. And the Baklava for dessert was as sweet as your lips." Best of all, a written response is something she can read over and over. You get big points for this.

*F*or those of you dating, a very big psychological acknowledgement must be given to anyone you sleep with, especially the first time. If you think enough of the woman to make love to her <u>even one time</u>, call her the next day and say something nice. Remember, you would do this for someone who invited you for dinner. This is sharing something a lot more than pasta. To do nothing leaves most women feeling emotionally scarred and insecure. Let's take a worst case scenario. Alcohol has accelerated the courting time to warp speed. You were "in lust" not "in love". You wake up the next morning knowing this is not a love connection. Pick up the phone, no need to lie about future encounters, just say something nice about what happened. She will get over it a lot easier with this gesture. Flowers sent to her home the next day are always appropriate. Hopefully if you are having sex, you are in love and involved in a meaningful relationship. In this case, you can never say it enough. Let her know you adore her. This will all come back to you.

Chapter 8

So What's in a Salary?

*M*oney or lack of it is no excuse for not coming up with a creative gift. Taking the same idea but applying it to different income levels will prove the point.

Gifts Guaranteed to Please a Woman

Photo

Student Salary:	Computer scanned or disposable camera shot framed in Lucite holder @ $5
Postman Salary:	35mm photo blow-up to 5x7 in a leather, wood, or brass frame @ $50
Executive Salary:	8x10 blow-up taken by a professional in a sterling silver frame @ $400
Trust Fund:	Photo session with the exclusive photographer Scavullo (you will need a connection to even get an appointment), Cartier frame @ $30,000

Flowers

Student Salary:	One perfect flower. Get the florist to wrap it in tissue and ribbon, or press/dry some wild flowers you both picked as you walked through the woods @ $9
Postman Salary:	Flowering English garden basket or gardenia plant, great fragrance @ $35
Executive Salary:	Exotic orchid which lasts for months, if chosen with unopened buds @ $60-$250
Trust Fund:	Extravagant arrangements from the best florist in town, delivered every week at home and at work @ thousands of dollars

Chapter *8: So What's in a Salary?*

Edible Treat

Student Salary:	Pint of hand-packed *Haagen Daz* ice cream of her favorite flavor @ $5
Postman Salary:	Half pound of *Godiva* chocolate @ $18
Executive Salary:	One pound of designer imported chocolate @ $40, a bottle of *Cristal* champagne @ $170 or three ounces of Beluga caviar @ $150 with a mother of pearl serving spoon @ $100
Trust Fund:	Custom box of chocolate, 50 ounces of Beluga caviar @ $2,500, case of *Dom Perignon* ($1,600), might as well throw in the *Baccarat* crystal glasses for the toast @ $300.

Gifts Guaranteed to Please a Woman

Lingerie

Student Salary:	Sexy panties, look for a sale (sexy to a college student could mean *Jockey for Her*) @ $10
Postman Salary:	A teddy from *Victoria's Secret* @ $50-$80
Executive Salary:	Silk gown and satin slippers from *Saks Fifth Avenue* @ $250-$300
Trust Fund:	Unlimited shopping spree at all her favorite boutiques

Entertainment

Student Salary:	Opening-night movie tickets, wait in line to buy tickets @ $15-20
Postman Salary:	Tickets to her favorite musical (orchestra section) @ $70
Executive Salary:	Season tickets to the ballet/sporting event @ $300-$3,000
Trust Fund:	Front row center box seats at the Metropolitan Opera House for the entire season @ $10,000, private audience with Pavoratti opening night (priceless). New haute couture gown of course.

Chapter 8: So What's in a Salary?

Trip

Student Salary: A drive to the nearest big city, (check out the freebies before you go - museum, exhibits, concert in the park, free lectures), dinner at an ethnic restaurant @ $40; if she's the outdoorsy type, a hike in the woods where you bring the picnic @ $15

Postman Salary: Package trip to Europe @ $1,500 (check your travel agents and newspapers for specials)

Executive Salary: Charter a 110-foot sailboat with crew to cruise the

Gifts Guaranteed to Please a Woman

	islands for one week. You can bring three other couples and split the cost @ $20,000
Trust Fund:	The Concord is fine to Europe but send for your own Gulf Stream IV for the rest of the trip. It's such a pain to fly commercially. Accept all the invitations from the VIP's you know around the world. They, like you, have so many vacation homes they probably will only arrange for the help to be there. Price will vary depending on your connections and tax write-offs.

Chapter 9

Saying "I Do"

The Ring

*I*f the answer to "Will you marry me" is yes, she probably doesn't care how big the ring is. The American Jewelry council reported that over 1 million engagement rings were sold last year. If you are a man about to give the gift that symbolizes the pledge of a lifetime, please consider all the general principals of *Chapter 1*.

- Have you been observant?

- Did you choose a ring that reflects her taste?

- Is she old fashioned where she might like to have your grandmother's antique ring?

- Would she prefer a traditional solitaire? (See Chapter 2 on Jewelry)

Gifts Guaranteed to Please a Woman

Timing

*T*iming is everything. If you only met her three weeks ago, maybe it's a little too soon to be 'popping the question'. On the other hand, if it has it been 10 years of courting (and she is foolish enough to have stuck around) she might have a coronary if you give her a ring without advance notice.

Presentation Counts

A small velvet box offered on one knee is hard to beat. Alternative hiding places include: sealed in plastic stuffed inside a turkey, hidden in a cocktail or baked in a cake. Complications can arise if

Chapter 9: Saying "I Do"

she swallows it. You don't want her seeing her ring for the first time in an x-ray. Whether the proposal is announced over television, sky writing, or flashed on a screen during half time at the Super Bowl depends on your imagination and her level of comfort.

Buy Quality

Be it diamonds or any other type of stone you purchase, buy the best you can afford. Don't 'cheap-out' on this, of all gifts.

The Element of Surprise

This adds so much fun when giving her the ring. Don't embarrass either one of you by asking her in a public place if you aren't absolutely sure the answer is yes. Let's assume the wedding goes well and you are now living in marital bliss.

The Gift of Life

The next big step is the gift of life. Okay, so you're not ready for the patter of little feet. Would little paws satisfy that maternal instinct for a while? Warm and furry pets opened at Christmas bring tears of happiness. One month later, however, reality sets in when that cute puppy is still not house-trained and has just ruined the new carpet; then, there are the vet fees, the walks in the freezing rain, finding a kennel for that weekend trip, and so on. This commitment is almost as complicated and time consuming as having and caring

Gifts Guaranteed to Please a Woman

for a baby. Maybe rethink that gift and substitute with a stuffed toy animal.

Having a Baby

*I*t is assumed you have given her the gift of your presence throughout the pregnancy including attendance at Lamaze classes. When the big day arrives, document the day. Remember to save the newspapers, cut out photos from magazines of styles of clothing, cars, etc. Take candid shots of the new mother, nurses, visiting

Chapter 9: Saying "I Do"

relatives, friends, and doctors. Cut out the top ten lists of books, movies and songs. This is a very thoughtful gift that can later be made into an album.

*R*ecognizing the occasion with a gift of jewelry is always appropriate, whether it is one pearl, a string of pearls, a guard ring to wear with her wedding band or a big bauble from your family estate jewels. A love letter expressing your joy, given alone or with another gift is a wonderful keepsake for any new mother.

The Eternal Gift

Let's assume everything goes well and you're enjoying wedded bliss. It's time to wrap up that lifetime commitment with the eternal present of a will. That's right, a will is a present to tie up the loose ends. Why should the state get everything because you were too lazy to get this done? It's a way of making sure your wishes are carried out and an obligation to your family is fulfilled. Doesn't your wife deserve everything? (Except maybe your prize fishing rod which you can leave to your buddy.) If you have children, be sure to discuss and appoint guardians. Set up a trust to provide for their future. Now you can rest in peace.

Chapter *10*: Times of Trauma

Chapter *10*

Times of Trauma

*Y*our gift of time, sympathy, and patience during life's difficult moments could be the most memorable and bonding. Antoine de Saint-Exupéry said it beautifully in <u>The Little Prince</u>, when he expressed his love for his 'rose'.

> *"But in herself alone she is more important than all the hundreds of you other roses; because it is she that I have watered; because it is she that I have put under the glass globe; because it is she that I have sheltered behind the screen; because it is for her that I have killed the caterpillars (except two or three that we saved to become butterflies); because it is she that I have listened to, when she grumbled, or boasted, or even sometimes when she said nothing. Because she is <u>my</u> rose."*

It is this kind of caring that builds relationships.

How to Deal with Illness

A woman is used to waiting on everyone else. If she is a typical female, she refuses to stop her schedule until she is on her deathbed. Joe, who claimed he worshipped his wife, was too busy to be at the hospital with her for a serious operation. His excuses included "it was an important golf tournament, good for business, great connections, after all, I'm the one who has to pay for the health insurance." Joe finally did show up with flowers he picked up in the lobby gift shop. His wife was still in intensive care. Her girlfriend had spent the night and was relieved to see Mr. Wonderful show up at last. Joe needed a reality check, and so did his wife if she put up with that behavior.

Let's say the illness is minor. She has a little cold or flu. You know how she waits on you when you are in bed with the sniffles. Play Mr. Mom and offer to change the sheets or throw in a load of wash. Hopefully, you have found your way to the laundry and know how to use the washing machine by now. How about making her dinner, if only opening up a can of chicken soup. Bring home her favorite carryout. Offer to go out and get medicine, extra tissue, hot water bottle (I saw one shaped like a lamb covered with fluffy fleece) anything to make her comfortable. If she begs to be left alone, do it.

Chapter *10*: Times of Trauma

A get well card and a few flowers wouldn't hurt either. It's only for a few days.

If it is a serious illness, don't disappear. You need to be her advocate and interface with the doctors. Picture yourself in a hospital emergency room with a broken leg. Would you be in any mood to fight with Nurse Ratchet who insists you fill out insurance forms before anyone will see you? I doubt it. You have been sitting in excruciating pain for three hours with no medical attention. Your leg is the size of a small tree. Wouldn't it be nice to have someone playing the part of take-charge Rambo and grab that arrogant intern by the throat so you could get a pain killer? Absolutely!

If she is facing decisions on treatment alternatives for a life and death illness, you need to literally 'be there', at the doctor's office, the radiologist, or for the blood test. As a patient, possibly on medication, she may not have the physical or mental strength to research and make the best choices. You may even want to tape record the doctor's prognosis and suggestions for courses of treatment for her. When she comes home from treatment, don't let her lift, drive, or worry about day-to-day chores. Offer to bring in help. If your insurance will not cover it and you can't afford to stay home, call family or friends to help fill in. To not offer your time and emotional support during this crisis would be unforgivable.

Mortality

The passing of a loved one is always bittersweet. You feel a great loss but are reminded of all the good times and how that person changed your life for the better. If the woman in your life has lost someone close to her, the best gift you can give is support over time. Be a sounding board; let her show her emotions; share her pain; be patient. Insensitive comments are better left unsaid such as "stop crying and get over it."

Offer professional counseling. Couples who face those challenges together come out closer than they ever could have imagined. A good book to read on this topic is Element Guide to Bereavement: Your Questions Answered, by Markum.

Chapter 10: Times of Trauma

Final Thoughts

Courtship never ends; it is a creative process. We all need creative attention. I hope reading this book has given you some insights in giving gifts that please the women in your life. Keep this book as a reference. If you use only a few of the ideas, I guarantee an appreciative response. Once you see her reaction, you will understand the joy of giving. You could become a legend in your own time.

Gifts Guaranteed to Please a Woman

About The Author

Ms. Adams has led the life of student, professional, soccer-mom, and jet setter. In all those lives she noticed the subject of men and gift giving was discussed frequently by women and often with frustration. For the past five years Ms. Adams has conducted interviews with hundreds of women around the world, from nobility to nannies, in an effort to understand the problems and offer solutions. This book is the result of those interviews. Ms. Adams presently resides in Palm Beach, Florida.

If you have an interesting gift story and would like to share it, please write me at: P.O. Box 1186, Southport, CT 06890 or visit my website at: www.giftsguaranteedtoplease.com.
For additional copies contact: www.1stbooks.com.

Printed in the United States
76346LV00003B/266